Japanese Grammar for JLPT N5

Master the Japanese Language Proficiency Test N5

Clay & Yumi Boutwell

Copyright © 2019-2022 Clay Boutwell

All rights reserved.

Clay & Yumi Boutwell

Makoto Monthly E-Zine for Learners of Japanese

Japanese lessons and stories with sound files.

It's only a few bucks a month!

www.MakotoPlus.com

You'll get:

Download the Latest Makoto Issue | Weekly Lessons | Podcast Bonus Content | Reusable TheJapanShop.com Coupon | Monthly Freebie

INTRODUCTION

Taking the Japanese Language Proficiency Test is a great way to not only assess your Japanese skills, but also to give yourself a concrete goal for your studies.

Goals help increase motivation and motivation almost always results in progress. Also, by making plans to sit in a test (usually) in a different city, you are making a major investment of time and money. There are few pressures in life that can motivate better than time or money. That's why I always recommend signing up and studying for the JLPT for any serious student of Japanese.

HOW TO USE THIS BOOK

This book covers some particles, grammatical patterns, grammar concepts, and special words with grammatical functions. Every entry includes an explanation of the concept, how to use it in a sentence, and then one or more example sentences.

We will present most examples in the polite *masu/desu* form. While other less polite forms may be, in some cases, more common, we think beginners should stick with the *masu/desu* form.

We highly recommend reading each example sentence several times—even dozens of times. Learning isolated vocabulary may be useful, but learning vocabulary within a natural context (sentence) while absorbing how the grammar works boosts productivity. While you read (paperback, tablet, or computer), you may want to use your smartphone to play the MP3s.

We assume you are using a textbook for your regular studies and have some (if only a touch) familiarity with very basic Japanese grammar. If not, we highly recommend getting a textbook to keep your learning structured before proceeding with this book. At the very minimum, to use this book, you must have a solid knowledge of hiragana.

SOUND FILES

While you read an example sentence (many times), listen to it. This will help with memorization. We also recommend "shadowing" the text. Listen to the Japanese and then repeat it out loud. Pay attention to the pronunciation and intonation.

The download link at the end of this book includes MP3s for all the grammar points and their example sentences.

ABOUT CLAY & YUMI

Yumi was a popular radio DJ in Japan for over ten years. She has extensive training in standard Japanese pronunciation which makes her perfect for creating these language instructional audio files.

Clay has been a passionate learner of Japanese for over twenty years now. He started what became his free language learning website, www.TheJapanesePage.com, way back in 1999 as a sort of diary of what he was learning.

In 2002, he and Yumi began TheJapanShop.com as a way to help students of Japanese get hard-to-find Japanese books. Since then, they have written over twenty books on various Japanese language topics.

Yumi and I are **very grateful** for your purchase and we truly hope this book will help you improve your Japanese. **We love our customers and don't take a single one of you for granted.** If you have any questions about this book or Japanese in general, I invite you to contact us below by email or on social media.

Clay & Yumi Boutwell

Clay & Yumi Boutwell (and Makoto & Megumi)
clay@thejapanshop.com

@theJapanShop

https://www.facebook.com/LearningJapaneseatTheJapanShop

http://www.TheJapanShop.com

CONTENTS

Contents

- INTRODUCTION ii
- Chapter 1: Particles 12
  - が 13
  - は 18
  - は～が 21
  - を 23
  - に 25
  - で 28
  - へ 29
  - と 31
  - から 35
  - まで 37
  - や 38
  - も 39
  - か 40

の 43

Chapter 2: Verbs 45
〜ます 46

Transitive / Intransitive 48

て Form 52

です・でした 57

Chapter 3: Using Adjectives 59
Negative and Past 63

Chapter 4: ko so a do 68
これ/それ/あれ/どれ 69

この/その/あの/どの 71

ここ/そこ/あそこ/どこ 73

こちら/そちら/あちら/どちら 75

Chapter 5: Question Words 77
なに・なん 78

だれ・どなた 81

いつ 83

いくら 85

いくつ 87

どれ・どの・どこ・どちら 88

どう・いかが 89

どんな 90

どのぐらい 91

なぜ・どうして 92

なにか・だれか・どこか 93

なにも・だれも・どこにも 95

Chapter 6: Enders 97
ね 98

よ 101

わ 103

でしょう 105

Chapter 7: General Grammar Points 107
あまり～ない 108

N+をください 110

V+てください・V+ないでください 111

V+ませんか 113

N+をくださいませんか・V+てくださいませんか
....114

V+ましょう 115

N+がほしい 116

V+たい 117

～とき 118

V+ながら 119

V+まえに・N+のまえに 120

になる 121

にする・にします 122

もう 123

まだ 124

など 125

くらい・ぐらい About 126

だけ 128

しか 130

の as Pronoun 131

〜中 132

という 134

Chapter 8: Conjunctions 136
Conjunctions: And... 137

Conjunctions: But... 138

Series たり 140

Because 142

Chapter 9: Other 144
たち・がた・ら 145

Counting 1-10... 147

Counters 148

Days of the Week • Counting days and Months
.... 152

Time ~時 157

Also by Clay & Yumi Boutwell ..... **Error! Bookmark not defined.**

Download Link 167

Particles

Chapter 1: Particles

Particles are the small, non-translatable words that tell the function of other words in a sentence.

This section may be the hardest for you to grasp. Memorize the examples and, just know, it will get easier with time.

が

ABOUT:

■ が usually indicates the subject of the sentence. We say *usually* because sometimes that task is covered by the particle は (pronounced *wa*) and with certain verbs, が is used after the direct object!

There are the above exceptions, but here is a simple way to look at it.

が identifies **specific** and **new** information when the subject itself is unknown or in question.

は, on the other hand, indicates the overall topic of the conversation.

HOW TO USE:

■ **New Information:** *When the subject gives the listener new information, use* が.

Here is an example where we introduce a cat with が but switch to は when the cat becomes the topic:

昨日、猫<u>が</u>いた。

Yesterday, there was a cat (*ga*).

その猫<u>は</u>、茶色だった。

As for that cat (*wa*), it was brown.

In the first sentence, the cat, as new information, is introduced with a が. The cat is the subject and answers the unspoken question, "What was there yesterday?" But it is not the topic of the conversation yet. If anything the "topic" is "yesterday." You are simply establishing the fact there was a cat.

In the second sentence, the cat is now being described and therefore, it is the topic of the conversation.

Now that the cat is labeled as the topic, you don't have to keep mentioning the cat.

For example, this might be the next sentence:

可愛かった。 (the cat) was cute.

■ **Question Words take が:** When question words like 何 (what), だれ (who), or どこ (where) are the subject, they always take が.

> **だれ**がケーキを食べた？
>
> **Who** ate the cake?
>
> **何**がほしい？
>
> **What** do you want?

■ **Use が for Subordinate Clauses:** Since a subordinate clause is apart from the topic (は), use が unless there is a contrast.

> 私は、ビル**が**いたことを知らなかった。
>
> (As for me,) I didn't know Bill was there.
>
> [ビルがいた (Bill was there) is the subordinate clause and therefore takes a が.]

■ **Direct Object が:** In some cases が marks the object.

> 私は、猫**が**好きです。
>
> I like cats.
>
> [or rather: As for me, I like cats.]

In English, what we would consider the subject (I) is

actually the topic. What follows relates to this topic (whatever the topic—I—likes). And what we would consider the object (cats) could be thought of as the subject of the verb.

This happens with a transitive verb or adjective. ("Transitive" just means it can take an object: I bought [transitive verb] a computer [object].)

Some common transitive verbs/adjectives that usually take が are:

- 好き **(to like)**

  あなたが好きです。 I like you.

- 嫌い **(dislike)**

  私は、牛乳が嫌いです。 I don't like milk.

- ほしい **(to want)**

  日本の車がほしいです。 (I) want a Japanese car.
  [The topic is assumed to be the speaker.]

- できる **(to be able to)**

  スコットは、日本語ができます。 Scott can (speak/write/understand) Japanese.
  [できます means "able to."]

MAIN POINTS:

- Use が for new information

- Question words take が instead of は

- Use が with subordinate clauses

- が is used with some transitive verbs (takes an object) even though the word it marks would be considered a direct object.

は

ABOUT:

■ As mentioned previously, は and が are very similar. There are three main uses for は as a particle: *marking the topic, showing contrast, and adding emphasis.*

STUDY NOTES:

■ Oftentimes you can think of は as "as for ..." or "speaking of ..."

HOW TO USE:

■ **Marks the Topic:** *Use は to mark the topic of what the rest of the sentence is about or describing. This is normally placed at the beginning of the sentence.*

私<u>は</u>、サムです。アメリカから来ました。

I am Sam. I came from America.
[The topic (what the following is about) is all about

Sam.]

■ **Adds Emphasis and Contrast:** Use は to show contrast.

ペンをもっていますか？
Do you have a pen?

ペン**は**あります。でもノートがありません。
I have a pen, but I don't have a notebook.

The contrasting は can be thought of as "I don't know about other things, but as for ..."

Two more examples showing contrast:

彼**は**赤が好きだが、私 **は**赤は嫌いだ。
He (topic) likes red, but I (new contrasting topic) don't like red.

テレビは見ないが、映画は見る。
I don't watch TV, but I do watch movies.

Consider the following comparison between が and は:

すしが好きです。
I like sushi.

(the が is simply establishing the fact the speaker likes

sushi.)

すし**は**好きです。

(I don't know about other foods but as for) sushi, I like it. [This person is not known to like Japanese food in general and therefore the は stresses the unexpected intention: "contrary to what you might think..."]

MAIN POINTS:

■ は sets the overall topic, can show contrast, and can add emphasis.

■ は is mostly used for things the listener knows about. Therefore, question words (who, what, where...) cannot be used with は.

■ は takes over が when the subject is also the topic.

■ If there is a は and a が in the sentence, the は usually—but not always—goes first.

は〜が

ABOUT:

■ Continuing our look at these two troublesome particles, here is perhaps the most common sentence construction in Japanese.

HOW TO USE:

■ AはBがC。

In this construction, C tells us something about B and B tells us something about A, since A is the overall topic.

<ruby>私<rt>わたし</rt></ruby>**は**、おなか**が**すきました。

I am hungry.

Lit: As for me, I | stomach | empty

[C (empty) tells us about the state of B (stomach) and B (stomach) tells us something about A (It is *my* stomach)]

■ When the listener knows the topic (A), the speaker can drop it since B and C are the core information.

おなかがすきました。 (I'm) hungry.

Another example:

日本<u>は</u>、地震<u>が</u>多い国です。
<small>にほん　じしん　おお　くに</small>

Japan is a country with many earthquakes.
[lit. As for Japan (A) | earthquakes (B) | country with many (C) | is]

MAIN POINTS:

■ は almost always comes first

■ は is usually dropped once the listener knows what the topic is.

ABOUT:

■ This is the direct object marker. It is usually spoken as "o" in modern Japanese although originally it was "wo." Some native speakers do sometimes voice the "w" today. But as a rule, pronounce it the same as お.

It is not, however, a substitute for お. を is only used (in modern Japanese) for the direct object marker.

HOW TO USE:

■ **Marks the Direct Object:** *In English, we don't have a particle that shows the direct object. A direct object is the object that a transitive verb acts upon.*

A transitive verb is simply a verb that has an object. For example: I carried a book. ("Carried" is a transitive verb)

私 は、**本を**読みました。
わたし　　ほん　よ

I read a **book**

[本 (book) is the direct object which was read]
ほん

STUDY NOTES:

■ **Caution:** This particle is pretty straightforward. Just put it after the direct object. The main exception is with some verbs, が or に replaces を after what would be the direct object in English.

私(わたし)は、あなたが好(す)きです。

I like you.

[Here, あなた (you) is the object which 私 (I) likes. But as mentioned previously, が is used with 好き.]

私(わたし)は、あなたに会(あ)いたいです。

I want to see you.

[あなた (you) is the object which the topic, 私(わたし) (I), wants to see. Normally, the object uses を, but に is used with 会(あ)う]

MAIN POINTS:

■ を is almost always pronounced "o" in modern Japanese. But to type it on the keyboard, you'll need to press "wo"

■ を is replaced with が or に when certain verbs are used.

に

ABOUT:

■ This particle is used for several distinct purposes. As a simplification, you can say に is a **time, location** and **direction** marker. It also shows what the indirect object is (who or what the action is directed to)

HOW TO USE:

Here are a few of the most common uses for the versatile に.

■ **Time:** *Use に to indicate times or dates in which something takes place.*

<ruby>朝<rt>あさ</rt></ruby>の５<ruby>時<rt>ご じ</rt></ruby>**に**<ruby>起<rt>お</rt></ruby>きます。

I wake up **at** 5 in the morning.
[morning | 's | 5 o'clock | at | get up]

<ruby>日本<rt>にほん</rt></ruby>の<ruby>学校<rt>がっこう</rt></ruby>は、<ruby>四月<rt>しがつ</rt></ruby>**に**<ruby>始<rt>はじ</rt></ruby>まります。

Japanese schools begin **in** April.
[Japanese | school | April | in | start]

■ **Location:** Use に to indicate location of existence. In; at; on

<ruby>ここ<u>に</u>本<rt>ほん</rt></ruby>があります。

There is a book (<u>at</u>) here.
[here | at | book | exists]

紙<u>に</u>絵を描きました。

(She) wrote **on** a piece of paper.
[paper | on | draw]

■ **Direction or Movement Toward:** Use に to show movement toward something. To; toward

東京<u>に</u>行きたいです。

I want to go **to** Tokyo.
[Tokyo | toward | like to go]

右<u>に</u>まがってください。

Please turn **(to the)** right.
[right | to | turn | please]

■ **Indirect Object Marker:** Use に after the object receiving the action. Think of it as "to" or "for."

私は、お父さん**に**ケーキを買いました。

I bought a cake **for** my father.
[**Lit:** as for me, I | father | for | cake | bought]

先生は、生徒**に**日本語を教えました。

The teacher taught Japanese **(to)** the student.
[as for the teacher| student | to | Japanese language | taught]

ABOUT:

■ Like に, で has many uses and is equally important. We will look at で to *indicate **location** and **the use of something***.

HOW TO USE:

■ **Indicates location:** *Use* に *for location of existence* [ここにいる (I) am here.] *but for other locations,* で *is used.* "In," "at," "on"

日本<u>で</u>、勉強しました。

I studied **in** Japan.
[Japan | **in** | studied]

本屋<u>で</u>、日本語の本を買いました。

<u>**At**</u> the bookstore, I bought a Japanese book.
[bookstore | **at** | Japanese language | 's | book | bought]

■ **Indicates the use of something:** *Use で when using something to do something.* "By," "using," "in," "from," "for"

<ruby>車<rt>くるま</rt></ruby> <u>で</u>、<ruby>行<rt>い</rt></ruby>きましょう。

Let's go **by** car.
[car | **by** | let's go]

テレビ<u>で</u>、その<ruby>映画<rt>えいが</rt></ruby>を<ruby>見<rt>み</rt></ruby>ました。

(I) saw that movie **on** TV.
[TV | **on** | that | movie | watched]

へ

ABOUT:

■ へ indicates direction or movement toward a goal.

Very often に can be used whenever へ is used.

HOW TO USE:

■ *Use へ after the location or goal the action is moving toward.* To; towards

EXAMPLES:

Note: in the following examples, に could also be used.

日本<u>へ</u>行きたいです。

I want to go **to** Japan.
[Japan | **to** | want to go]

友達<u>へ</u>手紙を書きました。

I wrote a letter **to** a friend.
[friend | **to** | letter | wrote]

と

ABOUT:

- と is a particle that shows relationships. We will look at four different usages for this important particle. *And; shows relationship; quotation marker; conditional: if then...*

HOW TO USE:

- **And:** *Using と for "and" indicates you have a full list of items. This shouldn't be used for open ended lists. Place it after each item in the list. The と after the last item is usually omitted but can be said.*

私<ruby>わたし</ruby> は、りんご**と**みかんを買<ruby>か</ruby>いました。

I bought apples **and** oranges.
[as for me, I | apple | **and** | orange | bought]

フランス語<ruby>ご</ruby>**と**英語<ruby>えいご</ruby>が話<ruby>はな</ruby>せます。

I can speak French **and** English.
[French language | **and** | English | can speak]

MAIN POINTS:

- Placed after each item
- Usually omitted after the final item in the list
- Used only with nouns and noun phrases (lists of things) and can't be used to combine sentences
- Must be an exhaustive list (not open ended)

HOW TO USE:

■ **Shows a relationship:** *When someone does something with someone else or when something is paired with something else, use* と. *With; as; from*

私(わたし)は、ジム**と**映画(えいが)を見(み)ました。

I saw a movie **with** Jim.
[**Lit.** as for me, I | Jim | **with** | movie | saw]

と is common with verbs that require two people or things to interact with each other. Verbs like 結婚(けっこん)する (to marry); 話(はな)す (to speak); 似(に)る (to resemble); 喧嘩(けんか)する (to argue)

ジムは、先生(せんせい)**と**けんかしました。

Jim argued **with** the teacher.
[as for Jim, he | teacher | **with** | argued]

■ **Conditional:** *Use と to show if this than that. If; when; upon doing so*

洗濯をする**と**、雨がふります。

When (I) do laundry, it rains.
[laundry | doing | **upon** | rain | falls]

説明書を読む**と**、すぐ分かります。

If (you) read the instructions, (you) will quickly understand.
[instruction manual | read | **if** | soon | understand]

■ **Quotation or sound marker:** *Use と to end quotes or set off sounds or ideas.*

「おはよう」**と**、先生が言いました。

"Good morning," the teacher said.
[good morning | (quotation marker) | teacher | said]

> 📄 It can also be used to close indirect quotations, internal thoughts, or sound effects.
>
> いけない**と**思った(おも)ので、やめました。
>
> I knew I shouldn't, so I stopped.
> [wrong | thought | therefore | stopped]

And it makes sound words into adverbs.

子供(こども)は、ぱたぱた**と**走(はし)りました。

The child pitter-patter**ed** as she ran.
[as for the child | pitter-patter (of footsteps) | ran]

から

ABOUT:

- から can show **a starting point** (from; since), indicate **what happens after** some point (having done that ...), or **express a reason** (because of that).

HOW TO USE:

- **A starting point:** *Used with time and locations.* From; since

6時**から**7時まで。

From six to seven o'clock.
[six hour | **from** | seven hour | until]

私は、アメリカ**から**来ました。

I came **from** America.
[as for me, I | America | from | came]

ここ**から**駅までは近いです。

From here to the station is near.
[here | from | (train) station | until | near]

■ **What happens next:** *Since the starting point shows a state in the past, it is followed by how it changed.*

信号は、赤**から**青に変わりました。

The traffic light changed **from** red to green.
[as for the traffic signal | from red | to blue | changed]
(Note, in Japan traffic lights turn "blue" rather than "green.")

■ **Giving a Reason:** から *comes after the reason or cause and, if needed, is followed by the effect of that cause.* Because; therefore; because of that

愛している**から**。

Because (I) love you ...
[love | because]

あした、テストがある**から**、勉強しています。

Because I have a test tomorrow, I'm studying.
[tomorrow | test | have | because of that | studying]

まで

ABOUT:

- まで shows an ending point. *Until; as far as; up to*

HOW TO USE:

- **An ending point:** *Used with time and locations.* Until; by; up to

EXAMPLES:

<ruby>6時<rt>ろくじ</rt></ruby>から<ruby>7時<rt>しちじ</rt></ruby>**まで**。

From six **up to** seven o'clock.
[six hour | from | seven | **until**]

<ruby>家<rt>いえ</rt></ruby>**まで**<ruby>10分<rt>じゅっぷん</rt></ruby>かかります。

It takes ten minutes **to get to** the house.
[house | **until** | ten minutes | takes]

<ruby>私<rt>わたし</rt></ruby>の<ruby>車<rt>くるま</rt></ruby>は、<ruby>5人<rt>ごにん</rt></ruby>**まで**<ruby>乗<rt>の</rt></ruby>れます。

My car can hold **up to** five people.
[my | car | five people | **up to** | can ride]

ABOUT:

■ や is used to list two or more nouns or noun phrases.

STUDY NOTES:

■ It is not an exhaustive list. *And; such things as ... and ...*

EXAMPLES:

店(みせ)で、牛乳(ぎゅうにゅう)**や**パンを買(か)いました。

At the store, I bought milk **and** bread **(among other things).**

[**Lit.** at store | milk | and | bread | bought]

好(す)きな動物(どうぶつ)は、猫(ねこ)**や**犬(いぬ)**や**イルカです。

Animals (I) like **include** cats, dogs, **and** dolphins.

[**Lit.** liked | animals | cat | and | dog | dolphin]

ABOUT:

- も means "*too*" or "*also*" but it has other slightly different usages: *both A and B; even ...* (used for emphasis)

HOW TO USE:

- **Too; also; either:** *Use も after the word it modifies.*

  田中(たなか)さん**も**行(い)きます。

  Tanaka will **also** go.
  [Tanaka | **also** | go]

- **Both A and B:** *Use も after both included words.*

  私(わたし)**も**あなた**も**行(い)きます。

  You and I will **both** go
  [I | **also** | you | **also** | go]

■ **Even ...:** *Use も after the word you wish to emphasize.*

子供は、一つ**も**人参を食べませんでした。

The child did**n't** eat **even** one carrot.
[as for child | one | **even** | carrot | didn't eat]

It is often used to show surprise.

こんなに大きな船**も**あるんですか？

Such a large boat **even** exists?!
[such a | large | boat | **even** | exists | (question marker)]

OTHER FORMS:

■ **Some common words with** も：

私も me too;

あなたも you also

■ Here are a few common question words using this form of も：

誰も no one;

何も nothing

か

ABOUT:

■ Most likely, one of the first things you learned about Japanese grammar was か is an end-sentence question marker. It is also used to show alternatives and suggest uncertainty.

HOW TO USE:

■ **Question Marker:** *Used to indicate a question.*

今、何時です**か**。

What time is it now**?**
[now | what time | is it?]

■ **Suggests Uncertainty:** か *is added to question words to show uncertainty. some~* : いつか someday; どこか somewhere; 何か something

いつ**か**、日本のどこ**か**に行きたいです。

One day, I'd like to go **some**where in Japan.
[**some**day | Japan | to **some**where | like to go]

OTHER FORMS:

■ One common expression is かどうか (whether or not...). This is often used without the どうか.

宿題（しゅくだい）がある**かどうか**知（し）りません。

I don't know **whether or not** I have homework.
[homework | exists | (whether or not) | don't know]

Is the same thing as:

宿題（しゅくだい）がある**か**知（し）りません。

I don't know whether **or not** I have homework.
[homework | exists | (uncertainty) | don't know]

の

ABOUT:

■ The most common usage of の is to indicate the possessive. It is also used to nominalize (make noun phrases from verbs and adjectives).

HOW TO USE:

■ **Possessive:** *Shows a relationship between two nouns or noun phrases. The apostrophe S.*

これは、マイク**の**本です。

This is Mike**'s** book.
[as for this | Mike | 's | book]

The connection can be extended and nested:

これは、マイクの友達**の**本です。

This is Mike**'s** friend's book.
[as for this | Mike | 's | friend | 's | book]

■ の shows relationships and attributes of what follows:

くま<u>の</u>プーさん

Winnie <u>**the**</u> Pooh

[bear | (a specific kind of which) | Pooh]

■ **As a nominalizer:** *Think of it as "one" as in:*
*This is big. → This is a big **one**.*

昨日（きのう）、買（か）った<u>の</u>を見（み）せて。

Show me the **one** you bought yesterday.
[yesterday | bought | one | (direct object marker) | please show]

You can use this to point out something specific:

赤（あか）い<u>の</u>がほしい。

I want the red **one**.
[red | one | want]

Japanese Verbs

Chapter 2: Verbs

In this section, we will take a brief look at verb forms, verb types, and verb tenses.

This will not be an in-depth look at Japanese verbs. Please use this as supplementary to your textbook.

〜ます

ABOUT:

■ Using the ます/です form is the easiest way to make your Japanese polite. In fact, it would be best to use ます/です all the time. The dictionary form (or plain form) should only be used with close friends and family.

STUDY NOTES:

■ **Formal Form:** *Useful in most any situation. Add* ます *to the stem of a verb.*

Plain Form	Formal Form
食べる to eat	食べます to eat
車に乗る to ride in a car	車に乗ります to ride in a car

■ *Verbs in Japanese do not change whether the subject is singular or plural:*

<ruby>私<rt>わたし</rt></ruby>は、<ruby>食<rt>た</rt></ruby>べます。 I eat.

<ruby>私<rt>わたし</rt></ruby>たちは、<ruby>食<rt>た</rt></ruby>べます。 We eat.

HOW TO USE:

■ *Add 〜ます after the stem of a verb.*

■ **Inflection:** *Verbs are inflected (form is changed) with past or non-past tenses and affirmative or negative forms.*

EXAMPLES:

<ruby>食<rt>た</rt></ruby>べる to eat (plain form)

↳<ruby>食<rt>た</rt></ruby>べます to eat (formal form)

<ruby>車<rt>くるま</rt></ruby>に<ruby>乗<rt>の</rt></ruby>る to ride in a car (plain form)

↳<ruby>車<rt>くるま</rt></ruby>に<ruby>乗<rt>の</rt></ruby>ります to ride in a car (formal form)

Transitive / Intransitive

ABOUT:

■ While this topic may seem complex, familiarize yourself with the concepts and learn examples. Eventually, it will seem natural to you.

■ **Transitive verbs require an object:**
I *want* a dog. [*want* is a transitive verb that requires an object (dog).]

■ **Intransitive verbs don't require an object:**
I *sang*. [*sang* is intransitive and does not require an object]

STUDY NOTES:

■ In Japanese, the same verb can take both forms by changing its sound slightly to indicate transitive or intransitive. The good news is, you can learn two words for just a little extra studying. You only have to learn one kanji and the two verb forms usually sound similar.

TRANSITIVE:

■ **A transitive verb** indicates **the action is done by someone or something**.

In Japanese, these verbs are called 他動詞(たどうし) and take an object before the particle を.

Sentence Pattern for Transitive (他動詞(たどうし)) verbs:

Acting Agent は (or が) | Object を | Verb

With a transitive (他動詞(たどうし)) verb, the は or が marks the **actor** that causes the **action** on the **object**.

The を marks the direct object, the object the actor affects. In some cases, however, が marks the object. See our entry on が for more on that.

INTRANSITIVE:

■ **An intransitive verb** has the **action done but who or what caused the action isn't important**.

In Japanese, these verbs are called 自動詞(じどうし).

Sentence Pattern for Intransitive (自動詞(じどうし)) verbs:

Noun は (or が) | Verb

HOW TO USE:

■ Let's look at a verb pair that tripped up Clay as a beginner: 落とす (transitive; to drop *something*) and 落ちる (intransitive; to fall)

[Transitive] 私は、ボールを落とした。
I dropped the ball.
[Intransitive] ボールは、落ちた。
The ball dropped.

■ Now, let's look at a 入れる (to insert; to put inside—transitive) and 入る (to enter--intransitive) [Notice the sound change.]

私は、猫を家に入れます。 I put the cat inside the house.
猫が家に入ります。 The cat goes inside the house.

With the intransitive form (入る to enter) the subject is doing its own entering and therefore doesn't have an object.

MAIN POINTS:

■ With a transitive (他動詞) verb, the は or が marks the **actor** that causes the **action** on the **object**.

■ The を marks the direct object.

EXAMPLES:

Here is a list of useful transitive/intransitive pairs.

TRANSITIVE	INTRANSITIVE
出す to take out	出る to leave
入れる to put in	入る to enter
起こす to awaken	起きる to wake up
落とす to drop (something)	落ちる to fall down
開ける to open out	開く open (doors)
閉める to shut	閉まる to be shut
消す erase	消える disappear

て Form

ABOUT:

■ The て form of verbs and adjectives has many usages. It is used for simple commands (do something), linking sentences as a conjunction (and), and to show an action that is currently occurring (present participle *-ing*).

HOW TO USE:

Before we look at usage, let's first go over the verb and adjective forms separated by affirmative and negative tenses.

■ **Affirmative Verbs Form:** *Add て to the simple past tense of the verb. This form is surprisingly regular. Simply change the た ending to て and だ ending to で.*

食べた ate (simple past)

change the た to て

食べて **please eat**

読んだ read (simple past)

change the だ to で

読んで **please read**

■ **Negative Verb Form:** Add で to the simple negative form.

食べない to not eat

add で

食べないで **Don't eat.**

読まない to not read

add で

読まないで **Don't read.**

■ **Affirmative Adjective Form:** *For i-adjectives, change the* い *into* くて. *For -na adjectives, simply add* で.

high; expensive:

高い becomes 高くて

famous:

<ruby>有名<rt>ゆうめい</rt></ruby> becomes <ruby>有名<rt>ゆうめい</rt></ruby>で

■ **Negative Adjective Form:** *For i-adjectives, change the* ない *into* なくて. *For -na adjectives, you change the auxiliary verb after the adjective.*

not high; not expensive:
<ruby>高<rt>たか</rt></ruby>くない becomes <ruby>高<rt>たか</rt></ruby>くなくて

not famous:
<ruby>有名<rt>ゆうめい</rt></ruby>ではない becomes <ruby>有名<rt>ゆうめい</rt></ruby>ではなくて

STUDY NOTES:

■ **Simple Commands:** *Use the* て *form as a way to utter a command. If this is too direct, add* ください *to make it more polite.*

ケーキを<ruby>食<rt>た</rt></ruby>べてください。 Please eat the cake.

スーパーに<ruby>行<rt>い</rt></ruby>って。 Go to the supermarket.

And here are examples of how to command someone to **not** do something:

ケーキを食べないでください。 Please do not eat the cake.

スーパーに行かないで。 Don't go to the supermarket.

■ **Linking Sentences (conjunction):** *It can also be used as a conjunction "and" or "and then..."*

私は、映画館に行って、友達と会いました。

I went to the movies and met a friend.

I could have written that as two sentences:

私は、映画館に行きました。友達と会いました。

But combining them with the て form sounds more natural.

Another example:

家に帰って、ビールを飲みました。

I returned home and drank a beer.
[home | returning | beer | drank]

And here are two more examples using the negative form:

晩ご飯を食べないで、寝ました。

I went to bed without eating supper.
[supper | not eating | slept]

切符は高くなくて、買いやすいです。

The tickets are not expensive and easy to buy.
[ticket | not expensive and | easy to buy]

■ Present Participle—Action is Currently Occurring:

This is the -ing form. This is used with いる *or the more polite version* います *(to be) after the -*て *form to indicate continuing action. What are you doing now?*

今、日本語を勉強しています。

Now, (I) am studying Japanese.
[しています is the て form of する (to do) and
いる (to exist; to continue)]

まだ (not yet) is often used with the negative:

まだ郵便が届いていません。

The mail hasn't arrived yet.
[as of yet | mail | not arrived]

です・でした

ABOUT:

■ です is a copula and also shows existence. A copula links the subject of a sentence with an expression that describes or renames the subject. In English, this is "to be."

One function of です is like an equal sign.

　　　　クレイ<u>です</u>。　"I **am** Clay." [I = Clay]

　これは、本<u>です</u>。　"This **is** a book." [this = book]

It also describes some property or state of the subject.

　　　　この猫は、白い<u>です</u>。

This cat **is** white.
[white describes the cat.]

HOW TO USE:

■ There are two forms: polite and informal, each with negative and past forms.

	Polite	Informal
Non-past	です	だ
Non-past Negative	ではありません or じゃありません	ではない or じゃない
Past	でした	だった
Past Negative	ではありませんでした or じゃありませんでした	ではなかった or じゃなかった

Japanese Adjectives

Chapter 3: Using Adjectives

Unlike English, Japanese adjectives change depending on past or non-past and affirmative or negative.

Adjectives

■ In Japanese, there are two types of adjectives: い adjectives and な adjectives. The い adjectives are easy to recognize because they end with い.

■ な adjectives are everything else. There are a few な adjectives that end in い like きれい (pretty) and きらい (dislike). Memorize those two exceptions.

■ **Examples: い adjectives**

暑い（あつ）	hot
高い（たか）	expensive; high
おいしい	delicious

■ **Examples: な adjectives [Add the な before nouns]**

| 静か（しず） | quiet |
| 簡単（かんたん） | easy |

親切(しんせつ)	kind

Adjectives are their very best when modifying nouns. Let's see how to do that with い and な adjectives.

■ **Examples with Nouns: い adjectives [Simply add a noun]**

暑(あつ)い日(ひ)	a hot day
高(たか)いビル	a high building
おいしいすし	delicious sushi

■ **Examples with Nouns: な adjectives [Add the な before nouns]**

静(しず)か**な**ところ	a quiet place
簡単(かんたん)**な**テスト	an easy test
親切(しんせつ)**な**人(ひと)	a kind person

Adjectives in Japanese can turn into adverbs (used to modify verbs instead of nouns) by **changing the い to く for い adjectives** and **changing the な to に for な adjectives.**

■ **Adverbial Examples: い adjectives [drop い and add く before the verb]**

暑くなります	will become hot
高くなります	became higher (price or height)
おいしくします	to make (something) delicious

■ **Examples: な adjectives [drop the な and add に]**

静かに話します	quietly speak
簡単にできました	easily done
親切に言いました	speaking kindly

For the non-past tense, that is about it. Now, let's look at how to use adjectives in the past and negatively.

Negative and Past

ABOUT:
Making the negative for verbs and adjectives is fairly easy in Japanese.

■ **-na Adjectives:** *The adjective stays the same. Simply negate the verb. For* です *or* だ*, the negative is* じゃない *(or the more polite* ではありません *or* ではない*).*

元気です。 (I'm) fine.

元気ではありません。 (I'm) not well

[Or the **less** formal: 元気ではない or 元気じゃない]

好きです。 (I) like.

好きではありません。 (I) do not like.

[Or the **less** formal: 好きではない or 好きじゃない]

To make the past negative of a な adjective, simply drop the な and make the verb past negative:

元気ではありませんでした。 (I) was not well

好きではありませんでした。 (I) did not like.

■ **-i Adjectives:** *Replace the* い *with* くない *after the noun.*

うれしい happy ⇨ うれしくない not happy

> The only exception is the い adjective "good" いい. The negative is **よくない**. This is because いい originally was よい.

To make the past negative of い adjectives, remove the くない and add くなかった.

うれしくない	うれしくなかった
not happy	was not happy
おいしくない	おいしくなかった
not delicious	was not delicious
大きくない	大きくなかった
not big	was not big

Special Forms

ABOUT:

In English, adjectives are not conjugated. Delicious is delicious. But in Japanese, おいしい (delicious) can be:

- おいし**い** delicious (non-past; non-negative)

  ↳すしは、おいし<u>い</u>です。 The sushi is delicious.

- おいし**くない** not delicious (negative)

  ↳すしは、おいし<u>くない</u>です。 The sushi is not delicious.

- おいし**かった** was delicious (past)

  ↳すしは、おいし<u>かった</u>です。 The sushi was delicious.

- おいし**くなかった** was not delicious (past negative)

  ↳すしは、おいし<u>くなかった</u>です。 The sushi was not delicious.

- おいし**くて** delicious (て form)

  ↳すしは、おいし<u>くて</u>安(やす)いです。 The sushi is

delicious and inexpensive.

■ おいしく deliciously (adverb)

↳すしは、おいしく食べました。 (He) enjoyed eating the sushi. [He ate in a way that showed it was delicious]

■ おいしければ if delicious (conditional)

↳すしは、おいし**ければ**、食べます。 If the sushi is delicious, (I'll) eat it.

EXAMPLES:

Look at the following charts to see examples of the last three forms (て form, adverb, and conditional) for both い and な adjectives.

■ **い adjectives:** あつい hot | 安い cheap | はやい fast; early

て form	Adverb	Conditional (if)
暑くて hot and	暑く hot(ly)	暑ければ if hot
安くて cheap and	安く cheaply	安ければ if cheap
速くて	速く	速ければ

fast and	quickly	if fast

■ **な adjectives:** へん strange | 簡単(かんたん) easy | 静(しず)か quiet

て form	Adverb	Conditional (if)
へんで strange and	へんに strangely	へんなら if strange
簡単(かんたん)で easy and	簡単(かんたん)に easily	簡単(かんたん)なら if easy
静(しず)かで quiet and	静(しず)かに quietly	静(しず)かなら if quiet

Japanese Demonstratives

Chapter 4: ko so a do

The ko-so-a-do may seem difficult to grasp, but they are very regular. Learning them early on will definitely help with your progress.

The key is to understand the three positions:

1. Near the speaker [the "k" words]

2. Near the listener [the "s" words]

3. Away from both [the "a" words]

The fourth, "d" words," are the question words.

これ/それ/あれ/どれ

ABOUT:

These little words are called *demonstratives*, words like "this" or "that." While the number of them can seem daunting, once you learn the pattern, it isn't too difficult to sort out.

> These are sometimes referred to as "ko-so-a-do" due to the first hiragana in the pattern.

First, let's look at their use as pronouns.

HOW TO USE:

■ *Choose from three words depending on the distance from the speaker. The fourth word is a question word. This form is not attached to a noun but act as a pronoun.*

これ	This [for objects near the speaker]
それ	That [for objects near the listener]
あれ	That over there [for objects far from both people]
どれ	Which one?

EXAMPLES:

<u>これ</u>は、何(なん)ですか？

What is <u>this</u>?
[an object near the speaker]

あ、**それ**は、きつねうどんです。

Ah, **that** is kitsune udon.
[Uses それ because it is away from this speaker. Kitsune udon is a type of udon noodles with fried tofu.]

じゃあ、**あれ**は？

Well, how about **that over there**?
[an object far from both speakers]

<u>どれ</u>ですか？

Which one?
[This question word can be used for any object no matter the distance.]

この/その/あの/どの

ABOUT:

These mean the same as これ、それ、あれ、 and どれ. The only difference is these demonstratives must be attached to nouns. In English, we would translate both これ and この as "this," but in Japanese, これ stands alone and この attaches to a noun.

> 📋 Compare:
>
> This is a cat. **これ**は、猫です。
>
> This cat is black. **この猫**は、黒いです。

HOW TO USE: ■ *Attach to any noun.*

この+NOUN	This (something) [for objects near the speaker]
その+NOUN	That (something) [for objects near the listener]
あの+NOUN	That (something) over there [for objects far from both people]
どの+NOUN	Which (something)?

EXAMPLES:

この本は、面白いですか？

Is **this book** interesting?

[an object near the speaker]

あ、その本は、まあまあ面白いです。

Ah, **that book** is kinda interesting.

[Uses その because it is far from this speaker. まあまあ means "so-so."]

じゃあ、あの本は？

Well, how about **that book** over there?

[an object far from both speakers]

どの本ですか？

Which book?

ここ/そこ/あそこ/どこ

ABOUT:

By now, you should understand こ words represent something **close to the speaker**, そ words represent something **close to the listener**, あ words are **far from both**, and ど is the **question word**.

Now, let's look at location words. Where? Here, there, and over there.

■ **Form:** *Standalone words to show location.*

ここ	Here
そこ	There
あそこ	Over there
どこ	Where?

EXAMPLES:

<u>ここ</u>に住^すんでいます。

I live **here**.

<u>そこ</u>に座^{すわ}ってください。

Please sit **there**.

<u>あそこ</u>のレストランは、いいです。

That restaurant is good.
[a restaurant far from both speakers]

<u>どこ</u>のレストランですか？

Which restaurant?

こちら/そちら/あちら/どちら

ABOUT:

The last form of こそあど that we'll look at points out a direction. This way, that way, that way over there, and which way?

■ **Form:** *Standalone words to show direction.*

こちら	This way
そちら	That way
あちら	That way over there
どちら	Which way?

> 📖 A less formal way of saying these are:
> こっち、そっち、あっち、どっち

EXAMPLES:

こちらへどうぞ。

Please go **this way**.

そちらへ行(い)きます。

I will go to you (**that way toward you**).

トイレは、**あちら**にあります。

There is a bathroom **over there**. (Away from both speakers)

ご出身(しゅっしん)は、**どちら**ですか？

Where are you from?
[Literally, your origin-which way-is it?]

Japanese Question Words

Chapter 5: Question Words

Next, let's turn to a bunch of important but small question words.

なに・なん

ABOUT:

One of the most useful questions words is なに or なん. Both are pronunciations of the kanji 何 and both mean "what". So, how do you know which pronunciation to use?

> 📝 **Quick and Dirty なん:** *Pronounce 何 as なん if it comes before a word beginning with T, D, or N. For the most part everything else is pronounced なに. If this sounds complicated, just learn examples and you'll eventually get it.*

FOR EXAMPLE:

- <ruby>何<rt>なん</rt></ruby>ですか？ **What** is it?

[It is なん because it is before a "D" sound.]

- <ruby>英語<rt>えいご</rt></ruby>では、<ruby>何<rt>なん</rt></ruby>というのですか？ **How** do you say that in English?

[It is なん because it is before a "T" sound.]

This is a good rule, but here are a few other "rules" that

might be more concrete.

なに

Pronounce 何 as なに if it is by itself or before a particle. Also pronounce it as なに if before a noun (except when asking what day of the week).

- 何^{なに}？！ What?! [By itself.]
- 何^{なに}が好^すきですか。 What do you like? [Before a particle.]
- 何色^{なにいろ}が好^すきですか。 What color do you like? [Before a noun.]
- 何^{なに}もほしくないです。 (I) don't want anything. [Before a particle.]

なん

なん: *Pronounce 何 as なん before counters, when asking the day of the week (the exception above).*

- 何回^{なんかい} how many times [Before a counter.]
- 何枚^{なんまい} how many pages (of paper) [Before a counter.]
- 何曜日^{なんようび} what day of the week [The exception before a

noun.]

OTHER FORMS:

■ 何(なに)も nothing; not any [Takes a negative verb.]

↳ 何(なに)も分(わ)かりません。 I don't understand anything.

■ 何(なに)か something

↳ 何(なに)か飲(の)みますか？ Would you like something to drink?

■ 何(なん)でも anything; whatever; any

↳ 何(なん)でもいいです。 Anything is fine.

■ 何(なん)で Why? What for?

↳ 何(なん)で来(こ)なかったの？ Why didn't you come?

だれ・どなた

ABOUT:

The pronoun question word, "who," is primarily 誰(だれ) in Japanese. The honorific form is どなた. This is usually written in hiragana, but the kanji is 何方(どなた) (literally, what honorable person). Another honorific used in the same way is どちら様(さま).

> 📖 **Usage Tip:** Use どなた both to show respect to the person with whom you are conversing and for the person you are referring to.

For example, you might say どなたですか？ when speaking to or asking about someone who is older or higher up socially. Also, in situations such as answering the phone or the door when you are uncertain who you are talking to, use どなた or どちら様.

EXAMPLES:

- 誰(だれ)が好(す)きですか？ Who do you like?
- 誰(だれ)でしょう？ Who do you think?

OTHER FORMS:

- 誰(だれ)も no one [Takes a negative verb.]

  ↳ 誰(だれ)も来(き)ませんでした。 No one came

- 誰(だれ)でも anyone

  ↳ 誰(だれ)でも連(つ)れてきてください。 Bring anyone.

- 誰(だれ)か someone

  ↳ 誰(だれ)か英語(えいご)が話(はな)せる人(ひと)はいますか？ Is there someone who can speak English?

いつ

ABOUT:

いつ means "when" or "how soon." It is almost always written in kana because the kanji, 何時, can also be read なんじ (what time?).

EXAMPLES:

ごはんは、**いつ**ですか？

When is the food ready?

優子さんは、**いつ**来ますか？

When will Yuko come?

OTHER FORMS:

- いつも always

↳いつも、ありがとうございます！ Thank you, always!

- いつもどおり as always; as usual

↳いつもどおり、ピザにしましょう。 Let's get pizza as usual.

■ いつから from when; when will it start?

↳いつから、会議を始めますか？ When will the meeting start?

■ いつまで until when

↳いつまで、アメリカにいますか？ How long will you be in the States?

■ いつまでも forever; for good; indefinitely

↳いつまでも、愛しています。 I will love you forever.

■ いつか someday; sometime; one day

↳いつか、日本に行きたいです。 I want to go to Japan one day.

■ いつの間にか before you know it

↳いつの間にか、お金持ちになりました。 Before I knew it, I became rich.

■ いつごろ about when; how soon

↳いつごろ、パーティーにきますか？ About when will you come to the party?

いくら

ABOUT:

いくら can be used for asking how many things there are, but it is most often used when asking how much something costs.

EXAMPLES:

この 車(くるま) は、**いくら**ですか？

How much is this car?

値段(ねだん)は、**いくら**ですか？

What is the price?

お金(かね)は、**いくら**持(も)っていますか？

How much money do you have?

OTHER FORMS:

■ いくらでも as much as you like; as many as you want

↳お菓子は、いくらでも取ってください。 Take as much candy as you'd like.

■ いくら〜ても no matter how (much or many) [use with the て form; takes a negative verb]

↳いくら泣いても、あげない。 No matter how much you cry, I won't give (it) to you.

いくつ

ABOUT:

This form of asking the quantity of something is used for asking generally "how many?" and also "how old?" residence

今年(ことし)、**いくつ**になりますか？

How old will you be this year?

飴(あめ)は、**いくつ**ありますか？

How much candy do (you) have?

OTHER FORMS:

■ いくつも many; plenty

↳ 空(そら)には、いくつも 星(ほし)があります。 There are many stars in the sky.

どれ・どの・どこ・どちら

ABOUT:

These ど〜 words are the question forms of the "this" or "that" words in Japanese, the demonstratives. While covered in the previous chapter, we are expanding on these question words here since they are so important.

HOW TO USE:

- どれ which one [pronoun]

↳どれが欲(ほ)しいですか？ Which one do you want?

- どの which [used before nouns or noun phrases]

↳予約(よやく)は、どの窓口(まどぐち)でできますか？ At which window can I make a reservation?

- どこ where

↳ホテルは、どこですか？ Where is the hotel?

- どちら which way; which direction; where [Or the shortened and very casual form どっち]

↳ご出身(しゅっしん)は、どちらですか？ Where are you from?

どう・いかが

ABOUT:

どう and いかが mean "how" or "in what way" or "how about ..." いかが is more polite, but they are interchangeable otherwise.

EXAMPLES:

気分（きぶん）は、**どう**ですか？

How are you feeling?

すしは、**いかが**ですか？

How is the sushi?

お飲（の）み物（もの）は、**いかが**ですか？

Would you like something to drink?

最近（さいきん）、仕事（しごと）は**どう**ですか？

How is work recently?

どんな

ABOUT:

どんな goes before nouns and means "what kind of ..."

<u>どんな</u>学校に行きたいですか？

<u>**What kind**</u> of school do you want to go to?

<u>どんな</u>アニメが好きですか？

<u>**What**</u> anime do you like?

OTHER FORMS:

Anything: *Use* どんなに *with* ても *to mean "anything," "anybody," or "any way." Place before nouns and end with the* ても *form of a verb or adjective.*

<u>どんなに</u>強くても、負けるよ。

<u>**No matter how**</u> strong you are, you will lose.

<u>どんなに</u>長くかかっても、この仕事は、終わらせます。

<u>**No matter how**</u> long it takes, I will finish this work.

どのぐらい

ABOUT:

どのぐらい and どのくらい are interchangeable. It means, "About how long?" or "About how far?" or "About how much?"

This is made up of どの (which or what way) and くらい (about).

EXAMPLES:

東京と京都の距離は、**どのくらい**ありますか？

About how far apart is Tokyo and Kyoto?

あなたの身長は、**どのくらい**ですか？

How tall are you?

どのぐらい難しいですか？

How difficult is it?

なぜ・どうして

ABOUT:

なぜ and どうして both mean "why" and are basically interchangeable. A third "why" is なんで which is used the same way as the other two but is more casual.

EXAMPLES:

<u>なぜ</u>日本語を勉強していますか？

Why are you learning Japanese?
[why | Japanese | studying?]

<u>どうして</u>、そんなに歴史に詳しいですか？

How come you know so much history?
[why | such an extent | history | detailed/well-acquainted with]

なにか・だれか・どこか

ABOUT:

か as a sentence ender indicates a question. When added to a question or existence word, it adds uncertainty: "some ..."

何 what	何**か** **some**thing
誰 who	誰**か** **some**one
どこ where	どこ**か** **some**where
いつ when	いつ**か** **some**day

EXAMPLES:

- 何か飲みたいですか？ Would you like **something** to drink?

- 部屋には、**誰か**います。 **Someone** is in the room.

- **どこか**に蚊がいます。 There's a mosquito **somewhere**.

- **いつか**東京に住みたいです。 **One day**, I would like to live in Tokyo.

なにも・だれも・どこにも

The も attached to these question words means "none".

何(なに) what	何(なに)も nothing; not any (followed by negative verb)
誰(だれ) who	誰(だれ)も everyone; anyone -or- no-one (followed by negative verb)
どこ where	どこにも nowhere (followed by negative verb)
いつ when	いつも always -or- never (followed by a positive or negative verb)

EXAMPLES:

- 私(わたし)は、**何(なに)も**持っていません。 (I) do**n't** have **any**thing.

- **誰(だれ)も**私の意見(いけん)を聞(き)きたくないです。 **No one** wants to hear my opinion.

- かぎは、**どこにも**ありませんでした。 The keys were **nowhere**.

- あの子(こ)は、**いつも**ゲームをしています。 That kid is **always** playing (video) games.

Japanese Sentence Enders

Chapter 6: Enders

Japanese uses particles to give information such as the topic, the object, and relationships between words. Sentence-final particles usually express the speaker's emotions, seek confirmation, or emphasize what was said.

Let's look at the most common enders.

ね

ABOUT:

ね is perhaps the most versatile sentence ender. It can indicate *emphasis*, *agreement*, or be *a request for confirmation*. Sometimes, the same sentence can mean very different things depending on how the speaker says ね.

HOW TO USE:

■ **Agreement:** *Use to show agreement with what someone just said.*

そうです<u>ね</u>。

That's right. (I agree with what you just said)

おもしろいです<u>ね</u>。

That (what you are talking about) is interesting.

■ **Request for confirmation:** *Use when you want to receive confirmation the listener agrees with you.*

あなたは、アメリカ人(じん)です**ね**。

You are an American, **aren't you**?

Let's put the two together. In the following dialogue, one person will make a statement and use ね to request confirmation. The other person will use ね to confirm and show agreement.

A: テストは難(むずか)しかった**ね**。

The test was hard, **wasn't it**?

B: そうでした**ね**。

It **sure** was.

ね is also often used to soften a request or an otherwise slightly harsh statement. It is a way to sound nicer.

勉(べんきょう)強して**ね**。

Please study.

飲(の)んだら、乗(の)らないで**ね**。

If you drink, don't drive, **okay**?

It can also be used to emphasize the truth of a harsh statement.

うるさい**ね**！

(You) are too loud!

As with anything, context is king.

> 📄 One more use for ね is to make sure the speaker has the listener's attention. This ね may be said at any point in the sentence and is most often heard on the phone when visual cues are not available.
>
> 昨日ね、スーパーに行ったらね、山田さんに会ったんですよ。
> Yesterday, you see, I went to the supermarket, and saw Mrs. Yamada.

MAIN POINTS:

■ ね is one of the most versatile sentence-ending particles

■ It can be used to soften a request, show agreement, ask for confirmation, or grab the listener's attention.

■ Think of it like "isn't it?" or "don't you" or "you know..."

■ Used in casual conversation.

■ The manner in which one says ね often conveys what is meant by it.

よ

ABOUT:

This sentence ender particle is usually used for **emphasis**. The speaker is fairly certain the information is correct. This can simply be to stress what the speaker is saying or it could be used to correct the listener's understanding: *contrary to what you may think...*

EXAMPLES:

彼^{かれ}は、パーティーに行^いかないでしょう。

Doesn't look like he's going to the party.

いいえ、行^いきます**よ**。

Oh, yes, he **is** going.
[literally: No, (he will) go.]

MAIN POINTS:

■ Cannot be used with a か question ender (it would contradict the assertiveness associated with よ)

■ The sentence ender ね usually indicates shared information, よ is usually for information the speaker assumes only he or she knows.

■ ね can be used after よ to mean, "I say X, don't you agree?"

今日は、楽しかったです**よね**。

Today was fun, **don't you think**?

ABOUT:

This sentence ender often indicates emotion, admiration, or just a feminine touch. If used as an assertive ender, it is weaker than others such as よ. In standard Japanese, it is used by women.

EXAMPLES:

<ruby>今日<rt>きょう</rt></ruby>は、<ruby>楽<rt>たの</rt></ruby>しかった**わ**。

Today was **a lot of** fun.

あの<ruby>洋服<rt>ようふく</rt></ruby>は、きれいだ**わ**。

Those clothes are **so** beautiful.

[<ruby>洋服<rt>ようふく</rt></ruby> are Western-style clothes. Meaning, most any kind of clothing other than traditional Japanese clothing like a kimono.]

MAIN POINTS:

- Used by women, implying a feminine friendliness.

- Moreature to show emotion or admiration than assertiveness.

- Used only with declarative sentences; it is not used with questions or the volitional forms (the 〜ましょう let's... form).

- It can be followed with another sentence ender such as ね (to ask confirmation) or よ (to show more assertiveness).

でしょう

ABOUT:

This is a polite form of だろう and indicates a conjecture by the speaker which is not based on hard evidence. *It seems; I think; probably; don't you agree?* It can be followed with か to indicate a question or prompting of agreement.

HOW TO USE:

■ **Conjecture:** *Used to express a belief that may not be known for certain.*

> 彼は、日本語ができる<u>でしょう</u>。
>
> I **think** he can speak Japanese.

■ **Confirmation/Softener:** *Use to ask for confirmation of information by raising the final intonation or adding か. It also results in a less direct way of saying something.*

> 彼は、日本語ができる<u>でしょう</u>か？
>
> **Do you think** he can speak Japanese?

MAIN POINTS:

■ Used after the informal verb or adjective forms

■ Used to show conjecture or ask for confirmation of information

■ Adverbs showing conjecture or uncertainty can be used with でしょう:

↪たぶん (maybe)

↪おそらく (probably)

↪きっと (certainly)

General Japanese Grammar

Chapter 7: General Grammar Points

In this section, we will cover the little words—the power words—that will help move your Japanese forward in a more natural way.

あまり〜ない

MEANING:

■ An adverb meaning, "not much" or "not very," あまり shows the degree of something is not very great.

HOW TO USE:

■ Use with negative verbs.

STUDY NOTES:

■ It is sometimes heard as あんまり.

EXAMPLES:

ジェーンは、**あまり**ケーキを食^たべませんでした。

Jane didn't eat **much** cake.

[Jane | as for | not much | cake | (direct object marker) | didn't eat]

日本語^{にほんご}は、**あまり**分^わかりません。

(I) don't know **much** Japanese.

[Japanese language | (direct object marker) | not much | don't understand]

OTHER FORMS:

- あまりにも excessive

↳あなたの態度(たいど)は、あまりにもひどいです。

Your attitude is inexpressively horrible.

MAIN POINTS:

- Means "not much"

- Used with negative verbs

- Also heard as あんまり

あまりわかりませ〜ん！

N＋をください

ABOUT:

Please give me (noun) [a polite request]

HOW TO USE:

- (the object you would like) + をください

STUDY NOTES:

- Simply add をください after any noun. ください is the imperative form of くださる which is the honorific version of くれる (give me...)

EXAMPLES:

リンゴを<u>ください</u>。

Please give me an apple.

あの本を<u>ください</u>。

Please give me that book over there.

V+てください・V+ないでください

ABOUT:

- Please do (verb) [a polite request]

HOW TO USE:

- (て form of verb) + ください

STUDY NOTES:

- Simply add ください after the て form of any verb.

To ask someone to not do something, use the negative て form: ないで and add ください.

EXAMPLES:

日本語を話してください。

にほんご はな

Please speak in Japanese.

ケーキを食べてください。

た

Please eat cake.

And a negative request.

話さないでください。

Please do not talk.

なにか、ください

V+ませんか

ABOUT:

Sometimes in English, to be polite, we ask questions in the negative. "Won't you take a seat?" Japanese does this often also for polite requests or questions. "Wouldn't you like?" "Won't you...?"

〜ませんか is used to make polite invitations or to give soft commands.

HOW TO USE:
■ Replace ます with ませんか.

EXAMPLES:

パーティーに来ませんか？

Won't you come to the party?

[来ます to come | 来ません don't come]

映画を見に行きませんか？

Why don't we go see a movie?

[行きます to go | 行きません to not go]

N+をくださいませんか・V+てくださいませんか

ABOUT:

Continuing our look at asking negative questions for politeness, using くださいませんか is a polite way to ask someone to give you something.

HOW TO USE:

■ Use as you would with ください. After nouns and after the て form of verbs.

EXAMPLES:

私の日本語を直して<u>くださいませんか</u>?

Won't you correct my Japanese for me?
[my | Japanese language | (direct object) | fix | won't you please?]

そのスーツケースを<u>くださいませんか</u>?

Won't you give me that suitcase?
[that | suitcase | (direct object) | won't you please?]

V+ましょう

ABOUT:

Using the ます/です form makes your Japanese polite. ましょう takes the ます and adds the "let's do" meaning.

HOW TO USE:

- Make the ます form of a verb and replace with ましょう

EXAMPLES:

どこかに行き**ましょう**。

Let's go somewhere.
[somewhere | let's go]

N+がほしい

ABOUT:

ほしい *is one of those words that takes a* が *particle after a word that is usually not the subject. What you want is the object. I want a cat. The "cat" is the object— what is being wanted by the topic/subject "I."*

HOW TO USE:

■ Say the object the subject wants and then add がほしい. You can add です for politeness.

EXAMPLES:

新しい車が**ほしい**です。

I **want** a new car.
[new | car | want]

秋田犬が**ほしい**です。

I **want** an Akita dog.
[Akita | dog | want]

V+たい

ABOUT:

Want to... Adding this to the ます form of verbs adds the meaning of *wanting to do that*.

HOW TO USE:

■ Drop the ます and add たい. You can add です for politeness.

EXAMPLES:

いつか、日本(にほん)に行(い)き**たい**です。

Someday, I'd **like to** go to Japan.

[行(い)きます to go | 行(い)きたい to want to go]

今晩(こんばん)、ピザが食(た)べ**たい**です。

Tonight, I **want** to eat pizza.

[食(た)べます to eat | 食(た)べたい to want to eat]

〜とき

ABOUT:

とき by itself means "time," but when used with a verb or adjective, it indicates a time when something happens or happened. "The time when..." or "when."

HOW TO USE:
- Add to the plain form of a past or non-past verb.
- Add to the plain form of a past or non-past adjective.

EXAMPLES:

あれは、若い**とき**の写真です。

That is a photo **from when** (I) was young.
[that | as for | young-time | 's | photograph]

食べる**とき**は、いつもテレビを見ます。

When eating, (I) always watch TV.
[eating | time | as for | always | TV | watch]

V+ながら

ABOUT:

ながら is a conjunction that indicates two actions are taking place at the same time. "While" "during" "as."

HOW TO USE:

- Replace the ます form of verbs with ながら.

EXAMPLES:

ポップコーンを食べ**ながら**、映画を見ました。

While eating popcorn, (I) watched a movie.
[popcorn | eating | while | movie | watched]

歩き**ながら**、携帯を使うとあぶないですよ。

While walking, using a cell phone is dangerous.
[walking | while | cell phone | use | upon (using) | dangerous | (emphatic)]

V+前まえに・N+の前まえに

ABOUT:

前まえに can be used both spatially and temporally.

In front of something (spatially) and *previous* to something (temporally).

HOW TO USE:

- Verb: Place after the plain, non-past verb.
- Noun: Place の前まえ after the noun.

EXAMPLES:

食た べる**前まえに**、手てを洗あらってください。

Please wash your hands **before** eating.
[eating | before | hand | wash | please]

仕事しごとに行い く**前まえに**、朝あさごはんを食た べます。

Before going to work, (I) eat breakfast.
[work | to | go | before | breakfast | eat]

になります

ABOUT:

になります is a useful tool for expressing "to become" or "change into." The plain form is なる.

HOW TO USE:

■ Nouns & な Adjectives: Simply place after the noun.

■ い Adjectives: Remove the い and add くなる or くなります.

EXAMPLES:

<ruby>来週<rt>らいしゅう</rt></ruby>、<ruby>私<rt>わたし</rt></ruby>は<ruby>四十歳<rt>よんじゅっさい</rt></ruby>**になります**。

Next week, I'll **become** 40.
[next week | I | as for | 40 | age | will become]

<ruby>彼<rt>かれ</rt></ruby>の<ruby>顔<rt>かお</rt></ruby>が<ruby>赤<rt>あか</rt></ruby>**くなりました**。

His face **turned** red.
[his | face | red | became]

にする・にします

ABOUT:

When deciding on something from several choices (e.g. at a restaurant), use にする or the more polite にします. Another similar and mostly interchangeable expression is にきめる, to decide upon.

HOW TO USE:

■ Add to nouns.

EXAMPLES:

<ruby>今日<rt>きょう</rt></ruby>の<ruby>夕食<rt>ゆうしょく</rt></ruby>は、ピザ**にします**。

I'll **have** pizza for supper tonight.
[today's | dinner | pizza | **decide on**]

<ruby>赤<rt>あか</rt></ruby>い<ruby>車<rt>くるま</rt></ruby>**にしました**。

I **decided upon** a red car.
[red | 's | car | **decided on**]

もう

ABOUT:

Don't confuse this with the shorter (in sound) も which means "also." This もう means "**already**" (something has *already* happened) or, with a negative verb, "**not anymore**" (done in the past but *not now*).

HOW TO USE:

■ Since もう isn't tied to a specific verb or noun, it can be used in various positions in the sentence, but it is usually at the beginning of the sentence. Also, with the "not anymore" meaning, finish with a negative verb.

EXAMPLES:

もう食べました。

(I) have **already** eaten
[already | ate]

もう酒を飲みません。

(I) don't drink sake **anymore**.
[not anymore | sake | don't drink]

まだ

ABOUT:

"Not yet" or "still." When まだ is used to describe events that have not yet occurred, it takes a negative verb. With affirmative sentences, it means, "still."

HOW TO USE:

■ There is some flexibility in location, but まだ usually occurs right after the subject or object whose condition *still* hasn't changed.

EXAMPLES:

青木さんは、**まだ**来ない。

Aoki **still** hasn't come.
[Aoki | Mr./Ms | as of yet | not come]

まだ、ピザはありますか？

Is there **any** pizza **left**?
[still | pizza | exists | ?]

など

ABOUT:

When you are giving a non-exhaustive list, use など as you would use "etc" in English. "et cetera" "and the like" "and so forth."

How to Use:

- Add after the last entry of a non-exhaustive list.

Examples:

日本、中国、韓国**など**は、アジアの国です。

Japan, China, Korea, **among others** are Asian countries.

新幹線の名前は、のぞみ、ひかり、こだま**など**。

The names for Shinkansen bullet trains **include** Nozomi, Hikari, Kodama, etc.

くらい・ぐらい About

ABOUT:

Approximate amount of something. ぐらい or くらい is used for asking "about how much" or "about how many." You can use it for estimating the number of things or time.

HOW TO USE:

■ Place after the object you are estimating.

■ It is used for estimating objects, time, and also as a pronoun.

EXAMPLES:

お客様は、どの**くらい**来ましたか？

About how many customers came?

[Here, くらい is used as a interrogative pronoun: *about how many?*]

Japanese Grammar for JLPT N5

ええと、１００人**くらい**来ました。

Let me see, **about** 100 people.

[Here, it estimates the number, "100 people."]

８時**ぐらい**に始まります。

It will begin <u>about</u> eight o'clock.

[Add に to show when it will begin.]

MAIN POINTS:

■ くらい and ぐらい are interchangeable and mean the same thing.

だけ

ABOUT:

When you want to limit how many or how much from a group, you can use だけ. Only; just; merely; nothing but...

HOW TO USE:

■ Place after the object or idea you wish to limit.

EXAMPLES:

試験(しけん)に落(お)ちたのは、私**だけ**だった。

Of those who failed the test, it was **only** me.

[私(わたし) だけ could be, "I, alone" or "just me" or "I was the only one..."]

もう一回**だけ**、あの山に登りたい。
<ruby>一回<rt>いっかい</rt></ruby> <ruby>山<rt>やま</rt></ruby> <ruby>登<rt>のぼ</rt></ruby>

I want to climb that mountain **just one** more time.
[Only one time; just once]

It can also be used for downplaying something's significance. *It's merely... It is only a...*

あの料理は、いいにおいがする**だけ**。
<ruby>料理<rt>りょうり</rt></ruby>

おいしくないです。

That food smells good. **That's all.** It doesn't taste good.
[It *only* smells good.]

しか

ABOUT:

Similar to だけ, しか limits to only one choice. Unlike だけ, you must use a negative verb with しか. "Nothing but..." Compare: 牛だけ "only cows" and 牛しかない "nothing but cows."

HOW TO USE:

■ Place after the noun.

EXAMPLES:

英語**しか**分かりません。

I **only** know English.
[Literally, "English-only-don't understand" but the negative should be understood in the しか. "I know nothing but English."

の as Pronoun

ABOUT:

You are probably aware of の as a possessive marker. の can also be used as a pronoun. In this case, it could be translated as "one."

How to Use:
■ When the context is understood, replace the noun with の.

EXAMPLES:

赤い**の**が欲しいです。
_{あか}　　_ほ

> I want the red **one**.
> [red | one | want]

先週見た**の**を買った。
_{せんしゅう み}　　_か

> I bought the **one** (I) saw last week.
> [last week | saw | one | bought]

〜中

ABOUT:

中 by itself means "inside" or "in." However, when attached to a noun, it adds the meaning of "during" or "while" or "throughout." It is either pronounced as ちゅう or じゅう. There appears to be no set rule for when to use either pronunciation. Learn a few examples by heart.

HOW TO USE:

■ Add to nouns or phrases to indicate duration or coverage.

EXAMPLES:

彼は、一日中、テレビを見ました。

He watched TV **all** day long.
[throughout]

仕事中なので、彼は外に出られません。

He is work**ing**, therefore he cannot leave.
[work-during-therefore-he-outside-cannot leave]

[during]

<ruby>来週中<rt>らいしゅうちゅう</rt></ruby>に、<ruby>宿題<rt>しゅくだい</rt></ruby>をすませましょう。

Sometime **in** the next week, let's finish the homework.
[next week-during-homework-let's finish]
[during a future time]

という

ABOUT:

This is used when you want to add a name to a description: "*such a* bird as that red one." This can be translated as "such a" or "called."

HOW TO USE:
■ Add after nouns and noun phrases.

EXAMPLES:

「アベンジャーズ」<u>という</u>映画を見ました。

I saw a movie **called** The Avengers.

青木さん<u>という</u>人は、いますか？

Is there **someone by the name of** Aoki here?

OTHER FORMS:

■ というもの something like that; something called...

■ ということはない nothing like that is possible; there's no such thing as...

■ というか or more precisely; or perhaps I should say; how should I put it?

Japanese Conjunctions

Chapter 8: Conjunctions

Here are a few conjunctions you will encounter on the test.

Conjunctions: And

ABOUT:

Let's look at the most common ways to join words and sentences. The following are equivalent to "and" or "also."

HOW TO USE:

■ と *to*—and

Used for joining words and phrases

私 は、りんご**と**バナナが好きです。

I like apples and bananas.
[I | as for | apple | and | banana | like]

■ そして *soshite*—and then...; also; finally

Often used to connect sentences but also can be used before a final word in a list: *and finally...*

車 をとめました。**そして**、窓を開けました。

(I) stopped the car **and then** opened the window.
[car | stopped | and then | window | opened]

Conjunctions: But

ABOUT:

As a particle, が usually indicates the sentence subject. Let's look at が as a conjunction that **combines two sentences to express contrastive thoughts**. In other words, "but."

While this is the most common usage, it can be used simply as a transition word to combine two sentences without necessarily contrasting.

HOW TO USE:

- Sentence 1 + が + Sentence 2

[Both sentences need to be in the same formal or informal form.]

CONTRASTIVE EXAMPLE:

スーパーに行った**が**、パンがなかった。

I went to the supermarket, **but** there was no bread.

Let's break that into two sentences:

スーパーに行った。 (I) went to the supermarket.

が **but**

パンがなかった。 There was no bread.

NON-CONTRASTIVE EXAMPLE:

映画を見に行きます**が**、来ませんか？

I'm going to see a movie. Won't you come?

In this case, you are using が as a softener. It is used to show you are casually bringing up the subject just in case the offer is rejected and you lose face.

Series たり

ABOUT:

Doing this, doing that, etc. This is for when you want to express a series of actions or states, but not list all possible actions or states. "Do things like ... and ... etc."

HOW TO USE:

Take the た form of a verb (simple past) or adjective and り.

- Here is how a verb is constructed:

立つ to stand

↳立った stood (simple past)

↳立ったり things like standing...

- Here is how an adjective is constructed:

高い expensive

↳高かった was expensive

↳高かったり was expensive and...

EXAMPLES:

立っ**たり**、座っ**たり**。

Things like standing **and** sitting

ドルが上がっ**たり**、下がっ**たり**する。

The dollar is **just** rising **and** falling.

今日は、買い物をし**たり**、レストランで食べ**たり**して、たくさんのお金を使った。

Today, I went shopping and ate at a restaurant, **etc**; I used a lot of money.

Because：から・だから・なぜなら

ABOUT:

Let's look at three words that expresses a reason or a cause. "Since" and "because." から, だから, and なぜなら.

HOW TO USE:

■ から

Verbs: *After the plain form (past or non-past) of the verb.*

よく勉強した**から**、試験に合格しました。

Because I studied hard, I passed the test.
[well | studied | because | test | passed]

い Adjectives: *Place から after the adjective.*

あのドレスは青い**から**、好きです。

Because that dress is blue, I like it.
[that | dress | blue | because of | like]

な Adjectives: Add the past or non-past plain form of です. だ or だった.

<u>あの絵がきれい**だから**</u>、買^かいます。

Because that picture is pretty, (I) will buy it.
[that | picture/painting-pretty/clean | because of | buy]

The next two listings don't connect sentences, but they do connect thoughts and show the reason or the cause of the previous sentence. "Therefore" "because of that" "so".

■ だから/ですから so; therefore

<u>だから</u>、気^きを付^つけてと言^いったでしょう！

Look, didn't I tell you to be careful!
[therefore | be careful | said | didn't I?]

■ なぜなら because of that

日本語^{にほんご}を勉強^{べんきょう}しています。**なぜなら**、いつか日本^{にほん}に行^いきたいからです。

Because I want to go to Japan one day, I'm studying Japanese.
[Japanese language | studying | therefore | one day | Japan | to | like to go | because]

Other Grammar

Chapter 9: Other

Let's wrap things up with a look at plurals, numbers, counters, and telling time.

たち・がた・ら

ABOUT:

These are plural markers for personal pronouns or proper nouns for people.

■ たち: *Useful in most any situation. Used with all pronouns except 彼 (he). Used with nouns and names of people.*

↳ 私<u>たち</u>

↳ あなた<u>たち</u>

↳ 彼女<u>たち</u> they (female) [彼 *he* takes ら in the plural: 彼ら *they*]

↳ 青木さん<u>たち</u> the Aokis

↳ 生徒<u>たち</u> the students

■ がた: This is an honorific plural marker which is mostly used with あなた and a few respectful positions and professions (mother, professor, teacher).

↳ あなた**がた** you (plural; respectful)

↳ 先生(せんせい)**がた** the teachers (respectful)

■ **ら**: This is the least formal plural marker. It can be used with humble and non-formal pronouns.

↳ 僕(ぼく)**ら** we; us [僕(ぼく) has a humble feel. You can use this with わたし but you wouldn't use it with the honorific わたくし]

↳ 君(きみ)**ら** you (plural) [君(きみ) is also humble. ら can be used with お前(まえ) but not あなた. This is used for one's peers or those younger than you, but not for those older or higher up socially.]

↳ 彼(かれ)**ら** they (male or mixed)

↳ 彼女(かのじょ)**ら** they (female)

↳ お前(まえ)**ら** you guys (a little rude/familiar)

Counting 1-10

ABOUT:

Japanese uses the Arabic numerals as well as kanji. Most numbers have more than one reading, one for the *on* reading (Chinese origin) and the other for the *kun* reading (native Japanese readings).

1-10: *The on reading is used for the cardinal numbers (normal counting pronunciation), so learn those first.*

Number	Kanji	On	Kun
1	一	いち	ひとつ
2	二	に	ふたつ
3	三	さん	みっつ
4	四	し	よっつ
5	五	ご	いつつ
6	六	ろく	むっつ
7	七	しち / なな	ななつ
8	八	はち	やっつ
9	九	く / きゅう	ここのつ
10	十	じゅう	とお

Counters

ABOUT: Japanese is full of counters. These helper words give information about the nature of the thing you are counting. Flat objects, people, small animals, etc have a counter.

Generic Counter: *Japanese does allow for counting up to 10 using the* kun *readings of the numbers. This can be used for counting most things.*

一つ (ひと)	1
二つ (ふた)	2
三つ (みっ)	3
四つ (よっ)	4
五つ (いつ)	5
六つ (むっ)	6
七つ (なな)	7
八つ (やっ)	8
九つ (ここの)	9
十 (とお)	10
いくつ	How many?

EXAMPLES:

<ruby>二<rt>ふた</rt></ruby>つありました。

There were **two** of them.

リンゴを<ruby>一<rt>ひと</rt></ruby>つ<ruby>お願<rt>ねが</rt></ruby>いします。

Please give me **one** apple.

HOW TO USE:

As we mentioned earlier, using counters gives us information about the objects we are counting.

- <ruby>人<rt>にん</rt></ruby> counter for people
- <ruby>歳<rt>さい</rt></ruby> counter for ages of people and animals; this is also written as 才; this is fairly regular except for age 20 which is はたち.
- <ruby>個<rt>こ</rt></ruby> counter for small or round objects [fruits; eggs]
- <ruby>本<rt>ほん</rt></ruby> counter for long, cylindrical objects [bottles; pencils; chopsticks]
- <ruby>枚<rt>まい</rt></ruby> counter for flat, thin objects [sheets of paper; stamps; plates; shirts]
- <ruby>匹<rt>ひき</rt></ruby> counter for small animals [cats; dogs; fish—usually up to the size of a dog. For larger animals, <ruby>頭<rt>とう</rt></ruby> is used.]
- <ruby>冊<rt>さつ</rt></ruby> counter for books

There are many, many more, but these are of the most useful.

Review the chart below and pay special attention to the <u>underlined</u> irregular pronunciations.

	人	歳・才	個	本
1	<u>ひとり</u>	<u>いっさい</u>	<u>いっこ</u>	<u>いっぽん</u>
2	<u>ふたり</u>	にさい	にこ	にほん
3	さんにん	さんさい	さんこ	<u>さんぼん</u>
4	<u>よにん</u>	よんさい	よんこ	よんほん
5	ごにん	ごさい	ごこ	ごほん
6	ろくにん	ろくさい	<u>ろっこ</u>	<u>ろっぽん</u>
7	しちにん ななにん	ななさい	ななこ	ななほん
8	はちにん	<u>はっさい</u>	<u>はっこ</u> はちこ	はちほん
9	きゅうにん くにん	きゅうさい	きゅうこ	きゅうほん
10	じゅうにん	<u>じゅっさい</u>	<u>じゅっこ</u>	<u>じゅっぽん</u>

	枚	匹	冊
1	いちまい	**いっぴき**	**いっさつ**
2	にまい	にひき	にさつ
3	さんまい	**さんびき**	さんさつ
4	よんまい	よんひき	よんさつ
5	ごまい	ごひき	ごさつ
6	ろくまい	**ろっぴき**	ろくさつ
7	ななまい	ななひき しちひき	ななさつ
8	はちまい	**はっぴき**	**はっさつ**
9	きゅうまい	きゅうひき	きゅうさつ
10	じゅうまい	**じゅっぴき**	**じゅっさつ**

> 📝 To ask, how many, simply add 何 before the counter:
> 何人(なんにん) how many people?; 何枚(なんまい) how many sheets (of paper)?

Days of the Week

Counting days and Months

ABOUT:

The days and months in Japanese are pretty straight forward. Let's learn the days of the week, the months, and then a few "special" words to expand our vocabulary.

■ **Main kanji:** 日 day; 週 week; 月 month; 年 year

■ **Days of the Week:** *You'll notice the ending stays the same:* 曜日(ようび)

日曜日 (にちようび)	Sunday
月曜日 (げつようび)	Monday
火曜日 (かようび)	Tuesday
水曜日 (すいようび)	Wednesday
木曜日 (もくようび)	Thursday
金曜日 (きんようび)	Friday
土曜日 (どようび)	Saturday

Names of the Month: For the name of the month, simply add がつ after the number. Pay special attention to the bold areas.

<ruby>一月<rt>いちがつ</rt></ruby>	January
<ruby>二月<rt>にがつ</rt></ruby>	February
<ruby>三月<rt>さんがつ</rt></ruby>	March
<ruby>四月<rt>しがつ</rt></ruby>	**April** **Note:** しがつ **not** よんがつ
<ruby>五月<rt>ごがつ</rt></ruby>	May
<ruby>六月<rt>ろくがつ</rt></ruby>	June
<ruby>七月<rt>しちがつ</rt></ruby>	**July** **Note:** しちがつ **not** ななmy がつ
<ruby>八月<rt>はちがつ</rt></ruby>	August
<ruby>九月<rt>くがつ</rt></ruby>	**September** **Note:** くがつ **not** きゅうがつ
<ruby>十月<rt>じゅうがつ</rt></ruby>	October
<ruby>十一月<rt>じゅういちがつ</rt></ruby>	November
<ruby>十二月<rt>じゅうにがつ</rt></ruby>	December
<ruby>何月<rt>なんがつ</rt></ruby>	Which month?

Days of the Month: The first ten days of the month have a number of unexpected variations.

ついたち 一日	1st (of the month)
ふつか 二日	2nd
みっか 三日	3rd
よっか 四日	4th
いつか 五日	5th
むいか 六日	6th
なのか 七日	7th
ようか 八日	8th
ここのか 九日	9th
とおか 十日	10th
じゅういちにち 十一日	11th
じゅうににち 十二日	12th
じゅうさんにち 十三日	13th
じゅうよっか 十四日	14th
じゅうごにち 十五日	15th
じゅうろくにち 十六日	16th

じゅうななにち 十七日	17th This can also be じゅうしちにち
じゅうはちにち 十八日	18th
じゅうくにち 十九日	19th
はつか 二十日	20th
にじゅういちにち 二十一日	21st
にじゅうににち 二十二日	22nd
にじゅうさんにち 二十三日	23rd
にじゅうよっか 二十四日	24th
にじゅうごにち 二十五日	25th
にじゅうろくにち 二十六日	26th
にじゅうななにち 二十七日	27th This can also be にじゅうしちにち
にじゅうはちにち 二十八日	28th
にじゅうくにち 二十九日	29th
さんじゅうにち 三十日	30th
さんじゅういちにち 三十一日	31st
なんにち 何日	What day?

OTHER FORMS:

Here are a few other words that are useful for telling the date.

- 何曜日(なんようび) What day of the week? [What "ようび"?]
- 先(せん) (previous): 先週(せんしゅう) last week; 先月(せんげつ) last month; [But, "last year" is the irregular 去年(きょねん).]
- 来(らい) (next): 来週(らいしゅう) next week; 来月(らいげつ) next month; 来年(らいねん) next year
- 毎(まい) (every): 毎日(まいにち) every day; 毎週(まいしゅう) every week; 毎月(まいつき) every month; 毎年(まいとし) every year

Time ~時

TIME VOCABULARY:

~時 hour [一時 1:00]

~時半 half hour [一時半 1:30]

~分 minutes [一分 one minute (notice the sound change: *ippun*)]

~ごろ about; around [一時ごろ around 1:00]

午前 A.M.; morning [午前八時 8 A.M.]

午後 P.M.; afternoon [午後八時 8 P.M.]

HOW TO USE:

■ **HOURS ~時:** *Add "ji" after numbers to give the hour of the day.* 時 *is the counter for hours.*

<ruby>1<rt>いち</rt></ruby><ruby>時<rt>じ</rt></ruby>	1 o'clock
<ruby>2<rt>に</rt></ruby><ruby>時<rt>じ</rt></ruby>	2 o'clock
<ruby>3<rt>さん</rt></ruby><ruby>時<rt>じ</rt></ruby>	3 o'clock
<ruby>4<rt>よ</rt></ruby><ruby>時<rt>じ</rt></ruby>	4 o'clock [note it is *yoji* not *yonji*]
<ruby>5<rt>ご</rt></ruby><ruby>時<rt>じ</rt></ruby>	5 o'clock
<ruby>6<rt>ろく</rt></ruby><ruby>時<rt>じ</rt></ruby>	6 o'clock
<ruby>7<rt>しち</rt></ruby><ruby>時<rt>じ</rt></ruby>	7 o'clock
<ruby>8<rt>はち</rt></ruby><ruby>時<rt>じ</rt></ruby>	8 o'clock
<ruby>9<rt>く</rt></ruby><ruby>時<rt>じ</rt></ruby>	9 o'clock
<ruby>10<rt>じゅう</rt></ruby><ruby>時<rt>じ</rt></ruby>	10 o'clock
<ruby>11<rt>じゅういち</rt></ruby><ruby>時<rt>じ</rt></ruby>	11 o'clock
<ruby>12<rt>じゅうに</rt></ruby><ruby>時<rt>じ</rt></ruby>	12 o'clock
<ruby>何時<rt>なんじ</rt></ruby>	What time?

■ **HALF HOURS ~時半**: Add after numbers to show the half hour. 半 means "half." You'll see this kanji in words like 半島 (peninsula—half an island) and 半額 (half price—a sale)

1時半

1:30

6時半

6:30

■ **ABOUT ~ごろ**: To show approximation, add ごろ after the hour.

2時ごろ

about 2 o'clock

[You can write numbers in kanji or with numerals.]

■ **MINUTES ~分:** *Add after numbers to give the minutes. While the pronunciation is* ふん, *it can also be* ぷん *depending on what number it follows.* 分 *is the counter for minutes. Pay attention to the bold variations below:*

ぷん	いっぷん 1分	1 minute
ふん	に ふん 2分	2 minutes
ぷん	さんぷん 3分	3 minutes
ぷん	よんぷん 4分	4 minutes
ふん	ご ふん 5分	5 minutes
ぷん	ろっぷん 6分	6 minutes
ふん	ななふん 7分	7 minutes
ぷん or ふん	はっぷん　はちふん 8分 or 8分	8 minutes
ふん	きゅうふん 9分	9 minutes [notice "*kufun*" isn't used]
ぷん	じゅっぷん １０分	10 minutes
ぷん	なんぷん 何分	How many minutes?

> 📖 The good news is, these patterns just repeat themselves. So, if you want 11 minutes, it is १ १分 (じゅういっぷん). And 18 minutes can be either १ ८分 (じゅはっぷん) or １ ８分 (じゅうはちふん).

Here are a few time examples:

６時６分 (ろくじろっぷん) is the same thing as 6:06. [Notice the second "6" has a small っ when before 分. "*Roppun*" instead of "*rokupun*."]

１時５９分 (いちじごじゅうきゅうふん) is the same thing as 1:59.

Note: １時３０分 (いちじさんじゅっぷん) is the same thing as １時半 (いちじはん).

■午前~: *Add <u>before</u> the hour to mean AM, the morning.*

午前１時 (ごぜんいちじ)

1 AM

午前１１時半 (ごぜんじゅういちじはん)

11:30 AM

■午後~: *Add <u>before</u> the hour to mean PM, the afternoon.*

<ruby>午<rt>ご</rt>後<rt>ご</rt>1<rt>いち</rt>時<rt>じ</rt></ruby>

1 PM

<ruby>午<rt>ご</rt>後<rt>ご</rt>1 1<rt>じゅういち</rt>時<rt>じ</rt>半<rt>はん</rt></ruby>

11:30 PM

> 📝 Note: Although you can use 午前 (AM) and 午後 (PM), 24 hour military time is often used in Japan.

Spanning Time
~時間/~分/~ぐらい

ABOUT:

Finally, let's look at expressing spans of time. How many hours (時間), how many minutes (分), and about how long (くらい・ぐらい).

■ 時間: *This means "time" in general as well has "hour."* You probably know how to ask the time and give it:

<u>何時</u>ですか？

What time is it?

1<u>時</u>です。

It is one **o'clock**.

But adding 間 (かん) (space; interval) gives us a **span of time**.

いつ戻(もど)りますか？

When will you return?

1時間(いちじかん)で戻(もど)ります。

(I) will return in **(the span of) an hour**

毎日(まいにち)、**2時間**(にじかん)日本語(にほんご)を勉強(べんきょう)しています。

I study Japanese **for two hours** every day.

■ 分(ふん): *This means "minute", a unit of time. As mentioned previously, the pronunciation is* ふん, *it can also be* ぷん *depending on what number it follows.* Here are the "*pun*" pronunciations:

ぷん	1分 (いっぷん)	1 minute
ぷん	3分 (さんぷん)	3 minutes
ぷん	4分 (よんぷん)	4 minutes
ぷん	6分 (ろっぷん)	6 minutes
ぷん or ふん	8分 (はっぷん) or 8分 (はちふん)	8 minutes
ぷん	10分 (じゅっぷん)	10 minutes
ぷん	何分 (なんぷん)	How many minutes?

As mentioned previously, these patterns just repeat themselves. So, if you want 11 minutes, it is １１分 (じゅういっぷん). And 18 minutes can be either １８分 (じゅっはっぷん) or １８分 (じゅうはちふん).

■ **くらい・ぐらい**: *This means "about", and, once again, the pronunciation can change depending on the speaker.*

Unlike 分, the sound change isn't standardized. While there were historical reasons for one or the other, today, the difference isn't clear and くらい and ぐらい are pretty much interchangeable.

２時間ぐらい (にじかん)

About two hours

テストは３０分くらいかかります。(さんじゅっぷん)

The test takes **about** thirty minutes.

USEFUL EXPRESSIONS:

■ 時間を潰す。(じかん・つぶ)
to kill time

■ 時間を無駄にする。(じかん・むだ)
to waste time

■ 時間がない。(じかん)
to not have time; to run out of time

■ 一日おき (いちにち)
every other day

Digital Bundles

Download Link

Please go to this website to download the MP3s for all the Japanese: (There is an exclusive free gift on kanji waiting there too)

http://japanesereaders.com/10245

As an extra added bonus, here is a coupon **for 10%** off your next order at www.TheJapanShop.com. Just use the coupon:

MATANE

(Just use the above word in CAPITALS; no minimum order amount!)

Thank you for purchasing and reading this book! To contact the authors, please email them at help@thejapanshop.com. See also the wide selection of materials for learning Japanese at www.TheJapanShop.com and the free site for learning Japanese at www.thejapanesepage.com.

Made in the USA
Columbia, SC
14 August 2024